CHILDREN'S ENCYCLOPEDIA
THE WORLD OF KNOWLEDGE

SPACE SCIENCE

Manasvi Vohra

Published by:

F-2/16, Ansari road, Daryaganj, New Delhi-110002
☎ 23240026, 23240027 • *Fax:* 011-23240028
Email: info@vspublishers.com • *Website:* www.vspublishers.com
Online Brandstore: *amazon.in/vspublishers*

Regional Office : Hyderabad
5-1-707/1, Brij Bhawan (Beside Central Bank of India
Lane) Bank Street, Koti, Hyderabad - 500 095
☎ 040-24737290
E-mail: vspublishershyd@gmail.com

Branch Office : Mumbai
Jaywant Industrial Estate, 1st Floor–108, Tardeo Road
Opposite Sobo Central Mall, Mumbai – 400 034
☎ 022-23510736
E-mail: vspublishersmum@gmail.com

BUY OUR BOOKS FROM: AMAZON FLIPKART

© Copyright: V&S PUBLISHERS
ISBN 978-9-3-505791-1-4
Edition 2021

DISCLAIMER

While every attempt has been made to provide accurate and timely information in this book, neither the author nor the publisher assumes any responsibility for errors, unintended omissions or commissions detected therein. The author and publisher makes no representation or warranty with respect to the comprehensiveness or completeness of the contents provided.

All matters included have been simplified under professional guidance for general information only, without any warranty for applicability on an individual. Any mention of an organization or a website in the book, by way of citation or as a source of additional information, doesn't imply the endorsement of the content either by the author or the publisher. It is possible that websites cited may have changed or removed between the time of editing and publishing the book.

Results from using the expert opinion in this book will be totally dependent on individual circumstances and factors beyond the control of the author and the publisher.

It makes sense to elicit advice from well informed sources before implementing the ideas given in the book. The reader assumes full responsibility for the consequences arising out from reading this book.

For proper guidance, it is advisable to read the book under the watchful eyes of parents/guardian. The buyer of this book assumes all responsibility for the use of given materials and information.

The copyright of the entire content of this book rests with the author/publisher. Any infringement/transmission of the cover design, text or illustrations, in any form, by any means, by any entity will invite legal action and be responsible for consequences thereon.

PUBLISHER'S NOTE

V&S Publishers is glad to announce the launch of a unique, set of 12 books under the head, *Children's Encyclopedia – The World of Knowledge.* The set of 12 books namely – *Physices, Chemistry, Space Science, General Sceince, Life Science, Human Body, Electronics & Communications, Scientists, Inventions & Discoveries, Transportation, The Earth, and GK (General Knowledge)* has been especially developed keeping in mind the students and children of all age groups, particularly from 6 to 14 years of age. Our main aim is to arouse the interest and solve the queries of the school children regarding the various and diverse topics of Science and help them master the subject thoroughly.

In the book, *Space Science*, the author has broadly dealt with some interesting and fascinating Scientific facts like *The Universe, The Stars, The Solar System, The Sun, The Moons, The Meteorites, The Comets,* etc.

Each chapter is followed by a section called **Quick Facts** that contains a set of interesting and fascinating facts about the topics already discussed in the chapter. At the end of the book a **Glossary** of difficult words and scientific terms to make the book complete and comprehensive is given.

Quick Facts

- We can see about 2,000 stars in the sky on a clear, dark night.

Though our aim is to be flawless, but errors might have crept in inadvertently. So we request our esteemed readers to read the book thoroughly and offer valuable suggestions wherever necessary to improve and enhance the quality of the book. Hope it interests you all and serves its purpose well.

CONTENTS

SPACE SCIENCE

Chapter 1 : The Universe 9

Chapter 2 : The Stars 14

Chapter 3 : The Solar System 19

Chapter 4 : The Sun 27

Chapter 5 : The Moons 30

Chapter 6 : The Meteorites 34

Chapter 7 : The Comets 38

Chapter 8 : Space Exploration 41

SPACE SCIENCE

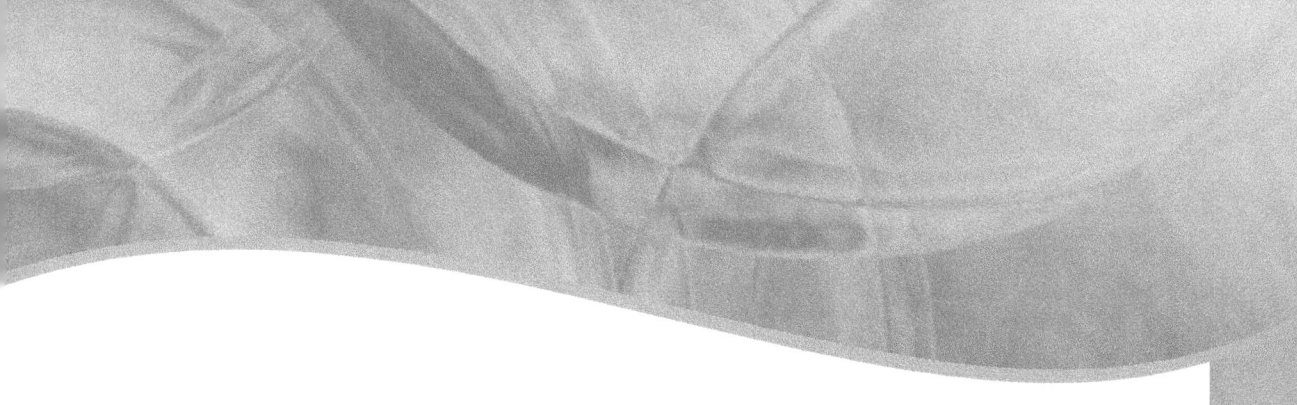

Chapter - 1

THE UNIVERSE

About 13.7 billion years ago, the Universe was formed in a massive explosion called the **Big Bang**. The Universe consists of everything that exists:

- Matter
- Space
- Time
- Energy

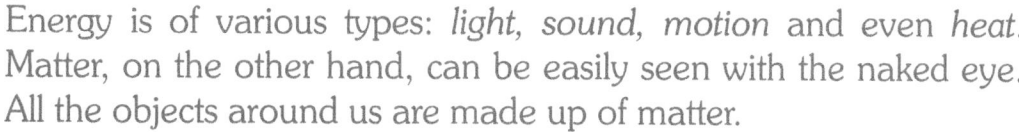

All of the above are parts of the Universe.

Energy is of various types: *light, sound, motion* and even *heat*. Matter, on the other hand, can be easily seen with the naked eye. All the objects around us are made up of matter.

Even today, the Universe continues to *expand, cool* and *change*. This phenomenon was discovered by the American astronomer, **Vesto Slipher** in the 1910.

Big Bang → 200 million years after Big Bang → Formation of Stars →

500 million years after the Big Bang → Formation of Galaxies → 1 billion years after Big Bang → Galaxies with different shapes exist in the Universe → 9 billion years after Big Bang → Formation of our Solar System

Big Bang

The Big Bang is the way the Universe began. It was not a sound, but an *enormous explosion* in which a large amount of energy was produced, causing the space to suddenly expand. This energy turned into matter on its own, forming the Universe. Astronomers (scientists who study the various bodies in the Universe) can tell that the Big Bang took place as some of that energy still exists and 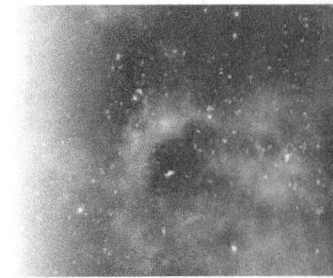 continues to fill the Universe with energy even today. This energy is known as the *Cosmic Microwave Background Radiation*.

Even though astronomers today have various explanations as to how the Universe developed from the Big Bang, they do not know what caused the Big Bang.

Galaxies

About one billion years after the Big Bang, galaxies were formed in the Universe. A *galaxy is a very large group of stars which are held together by gravity*

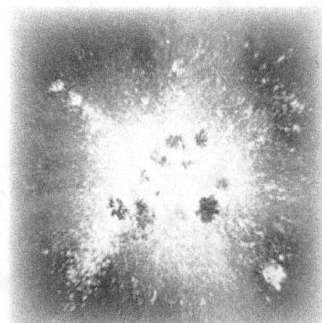

(a force that causes objects to fall on the ground). According to a scientific research, there are about 100–125 billion galaxies in the Universe. Each galaxy has more than 1,00,000 million stars.

Different galaxies have different shapes. Five basic shapes have been discovered till today. These are:

i. Elliptical Galaxy
ii. Lenticular or Lens-shaped Galaxy
iii. Spiral Galaxy
iv. Barred Spiral Galaxy
v. Irregular Galaxy

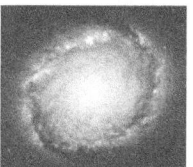

The Milky Way

The galaxy we live in is called the *Milky Way*. It was formed about one billion years after the Big Bang, at the same time as all the other galaxies. The Sun, the other Planets, the Stars and everything else are all a part of the Milky Way. According to astronomers, the Milky Way is a *spiral galaxy*.

The Milky Way rotates on its axis (an imaginary line through the middle of anything), faster at the centre than at the edges. The centre completes one rotation on its axis in about 50,000 years. The sun and its neighbouring stars revolve around the centre of the galaxy in their orbits at an average speed of 250 kilometres per second.

Andromeda Galaxy

Andromeda is the *closest galaxy to the Milky Way*. It is about *2.9 million light years away from the Earth*, which means that it will take us around 2.2 million years to get there, that also if we are travelling at the speed of light. This spiral-shaped galaxy can be seen from the earth without using any scientific instrument.

Edge of the Universe

Even though, early astronomers believed that somewhere beyond the stars, there was an end to the Universe, but studies have now proved that no matter how fast and how far you travel, *there is no end to the Universe.*

Size of the Universe

Even though, no study or research has ever been able to determine the actual size of the Universe, we know that the Universe is at least *90 billion light years across*. This has been determined by calculating the distance between the Earth and the most distant objects that can be seen.

End of the Universe

There are many theories about how the Universe will come to an end. Out of these, most scientists believe that the Universe will either continue to expand and cool, till it eventually becomes dark and dead or all the objects that make up the Universe, such as galaxies, stars, etc., will rip themselves apart. It could also happen that the Universe stops expanding and then crash into itself.

Quick Facts

- The name Big Bang was given by famous English astronomer, Fred Hoyle, who surprisingly did not believe in the theory himself. He was just making fun, but the name struck.
- Physicist Albert Einstein gave the mathematical model of the Universe in 1917. This model is still used today. The Big Bang Theory was suggested ten years later by Belgian astronomer Georges Lemaître.
- The Universe is also known as the Cosmos. Also, the study of the whole Universe is known as Cosmology.
- There are around 200 to 400 billion stars in the Milky Way.

Chapter - 2

THE STARS

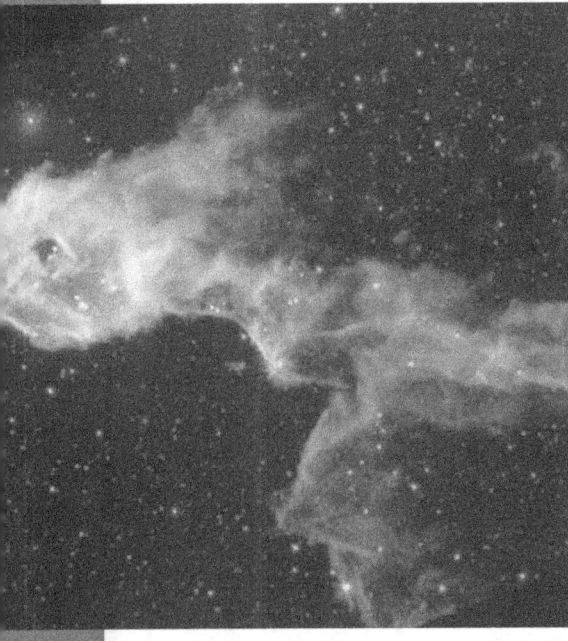

Stars are nothing but huge balls made of hot, luminous gases, which spin continuously. No two stars are the same. Each star has a specific temperature, colour, brightness, size and mass. These characteristics of the star change over a period of time, and hence, the star evolves from one stage of its life to another.

The life of a star depends on the amount of gas it is made up from, which is called the *mass*. Not only the lifespan, but also the characteristics of a star depends on its mass.

Life of a Star

Stars are born inside thick clouds of hydrogen gas in space called the *nebulae*. Clusters within the hydrogen clouds collapse inwards and are pulled together by gravity. They keep getting packed together and thus, keep becoming hotter.

Nebulae

Gas, along with little knots of dust are pulled inside the nebulae due to gravity. Each one of these could become stars as gravity squeezes it tightly and it becomes hotter.

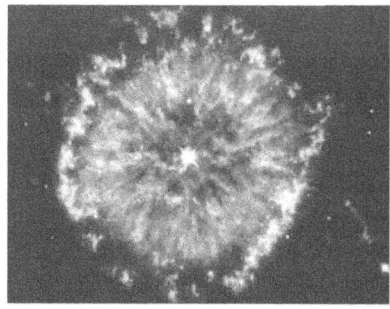

Red Giants

Stars are made up of *hydrogen gas*. Till the time they have hydrogen, they burn, after which they start to burn out. After this, they expand and become a *red giant star*.

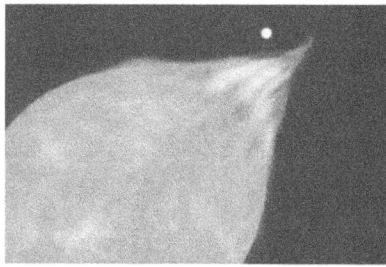

White Dwarfs

After some time, the outer layers of the stars are thrown into space. The only thing left is the cooling core. This is called a *white dwarf*. These white dwarfs are no bigger than the earth.

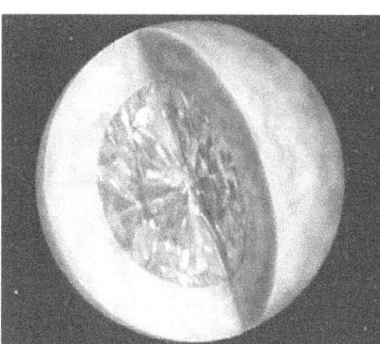

Supernova

The lives of massive stars generally come to an end with a huge *supernova explosion*.

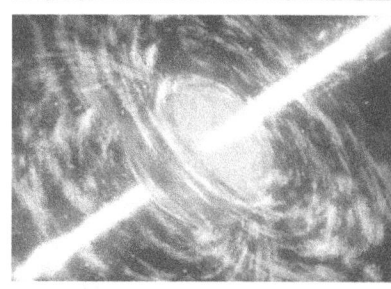

Remnants

A star's fragments or parts can remain in the space and continue to glow for hundreds of years.

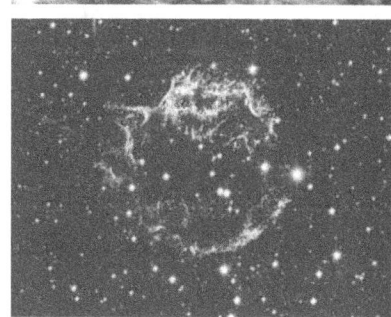

Stars in Motion

Even though stars seem to move at night, this is not true. It is not the stars, but the earth that moves beneath the stars, which are in space.

Types of Star Clusters

A group of stars that are close to each other in space are known as *star clusters*. This usually happens as these stars are formed from the same cloud.

Clusters that are round in shape and have many stars packed closely together, are called *globular clusters*. On the other hand, clusters which have fewer and more spread out stars, are called *open clusters*.

Biggest Star Found

Till date, the biggest star found by the astronomers is called **VY Canis Majoris**. It is about 1,800 to 2,100 times the diameter (the length of a line that cuts across the centre of a circular object from one end to the other) of the sun, which means that a billion objects, the size of the sun, can fit into it. It is also extremely bright, i.e., many thousands of times brighter than the sun. It does not look bright during the night as it is about 5,000 light years away from us.

Constellations

Constellations are patterns of stars in the sky. They were first used about *4,000 years ago.* Constellations are generally named either after a mythological creature or person, or after an object. Around

88 constellations have been identified in the sky till date. These help stargazers (people who study stars as an astronomer) find their way and navigate the sky.

The following are some of the popularly known constellations:

1. Gemini

2. Taurus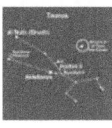

3. Canis Minor and Major

4. Monoceros

5. Orion

6. Eridanus

7. Puppis

8. Lepus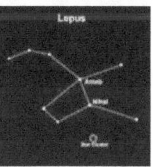

Quick Facts

- We can see about 2,000 stars in the sky on a clear, dark night.
- A star is a colossal, glowing ball of plasma and the star that is nearest to the earth is the Sun.
- Stars, including the Sun, have spots on their surfaces – sometimes enormous ones. Spots are cooler areas. They are caused by powerful magnetic fields.
- Hydrogen is the primary building block of stars.
- Stars may occur in many sizes, which are classified in a range from dwarfs to super giants. Super giants may have radii a thousand times larger than that of our own Sun.
- The colour of Stars can range from red to white to blue. Red is the coolest colour; that's a star with less than 3,500 Kelvin temperature. Stars like our Sun are yellowish white and have an average temperature of around 6,000 Kelvin. The hottest stars are blue, which correspond to surface temperatures above 12,000 Kelvin.

THE SOLAR SYSTEM

The Solar System is a small part of the space. It consists of the Sun, the Eight Planets, and innumerable other smaller objects.

In the beginning, the Solar System was nothing but a *huge cloud of dust and gas*. When it collapsed, pulled together by its gravity,

part of it became very dense and hot, turning into the Sun. All the materials that were left settled into a spinning disc around the Sun, where the planets and other objects that make up the Solar System formed.

The Solar System is enormous. Our Earth is just a tiny part of it. The closest natural object to the Earth is the Moon. As it orbits the earth, its distance from the earth also keeps on changing. At its furthest point, it is about 4,05,696 kilometres (2,52,088 miles) from the earth, while at its closest point, it is around 3,63,104 kilometres (2,25,622 miles) from the earth. Neptune is the farthest planet in our Solar System and its distance is about 4.5 billion kilometres (2.8 billion miles) from the sun.

The Solar System is not static and is constantly changing. Other than forming planets, some of the materials that formed the Solar System remained as *asteroids*, *comets*, and *other small bodies*. Till about 3.8 billion years ago, these objects quite often collided with the planets, due to which *craters* were formed. Even though the number of such collisions has drastically reduced, they still happen.

Planets

There are **eight planets** in the *Solar System*:
  (i) Mercury
  (ii) Venus
  (iii) Earth
  (iv) Mars
  (v) Jupiter
  (vi) Saturn
  (vii) Uranus
  (viii) Neptune

Mercury is the closest to the sun, while Neptune is the farthest. All the planets orbit the sun in the same direction. *Mercury, Venus, Earth and Mars* are completely made up of rocks while *Jupiter, Saturn, Uranus* and *Neptune* are made up of various gases. Due to this, they are also known as gas planets. As the planets go farther away from the sun, the time they take to orbit or move around the sun once, also increases. This happens because their distance from the sun increases. If we calculate in terms of the days on the planet, Earth, *Mercury only takes 88 days to complete one round around the sun, while Neptune takes about 64.8 years.*

Mercury

Made up of rocks and covered with innumerable impact craters, Mercury is a **dry planet**. It is the smallest planet of our Solar System. As it is the closest to the sun, it has the widest temperature range. Mercury is baking hot during the day, but freezing cold at night. Even though, it is difficult to see it without a telescope, (an instrument with lenses in it that help make distant objects look nearer) during the day due to its nearness to the sun and its small size, *Mercury can be easily spotted before sunrise or after sunset.*

Data	Mercury
Diameter	4.875 km
	(3,029 miles)
Average distance from the sun	57.9 million km
	(36 million miles)
Rotation period	58.6 days
Orbital period	88 days

Venus

Venus is the second planet from the sun. It is not only the hottest, but also the brightest planet in the Solar System. It is made up of rocks and is always surrounded by a thick cloud that traps heat and makes it a *gloomy planet*.

Data	Venus
Diameter	12,104 km
	(7,521 miles)
Average distance from the sun	108.2 million km
	(67.2 million miles)
Rotation period	243 days
Orbital period	224.7 days

Earth

Out of the eight planets in our Solar System, the *Earth is the only planet that has life and liquid water*. Third from the sun, the Earth is the largest planet that is made of rocks. The surface of the Earth continues to change due to the movements in its crust. The Earth also has one natural satellite, called the Moon.

Data	Earth
Diameter	12,756 km
	(7,928 miles)
Average distance from the sun	149.6 million km
	(93 million miles)
Rotation period	23.93 hours
Orbital period	365.26 days

Mars

Mars is also known as the **red planet**. Out of all the rocky planets, it is the farthest from the sun and is *extremely dry and cold*. Its surface contains *deep canyons, frozen deserts, giant volcanoes* and *polar ice caps*. These have all been formed in the distant past. It also has *two moons*.

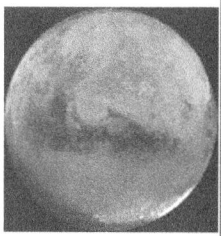

Data	Mars
Diameter	6,780 km (4,213 miles)
Average distance from the sun	227.9 million km (141.6 million miles)
Rotation period	24.62 hours
Orbital period	687 days

Jupiter

Jupiter is the *largest planet in our Solar System*. Not only is it the largest planet, but it also *spins the fastest*, completing one rotation on its own axis in less than 10 Earth hours. It is mostly made up of *helium* and *hydrogen*, but has a central *rocky core*. Jupiter also has a *ring around* it, which is very thin and faint. It also has a large *family of moons*.

Data	Jupiter
Diameter	1,42,984 km (88,846 miles)
Average distance from the sun	778.3 million km (483.6 million miles)
Rotation period	9.93 hours
Orbital period	11.86 years

Saturn

Saturn is the *second largest planet* in the Solar System. It is *pale yellow in colour* and is mainly made up of helium and hydrogen. Saturn also has a rocky core. It has a large family of moons and its distinctive feature is that it has a *ring system* which is made of innumerable pieces of dirty water and ice.

Data	Saturn
Diameter	1,20,536 km
	(74,898 miles)
Average distance from the sun	1,431 million km
	(889.8 million miles)
Rotation period	10.65 hours
Orbital period	29.37 years

Uranus

Uranus is the *seventh planet from the sun*. Its distance is nineteen times the distance of the sun from the earth. It is extremely cold and has a sparse ring system which encircles its equator (an imaginary line that cuts through the centre of the earth). It is an almost *featureless system world* bounded by a *layer of haze*. As Uranus is tilted on its side, it appears as if its rings and moons orbit it from top to bottom.

Data	Uranus
Diameter	51,118 km
	(31,763 miles)

Average distance from the sun	2,877 million km
	(1,788 million miles)
Rotation period	17.24 hours
Orbital period	84.1 years

Neptune

Out of the eight planets in our Solar System, the **Neptune is the farthest**. It is also the windiest and the coldest. Its atmosphere consists of hydrogen-rich gas and the planet itself is basically made up of ammonia, methane and water ices. Neptune also has an extremely thin ring system and a large family of moons.

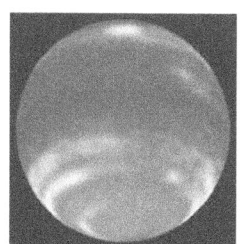

Data	Neptune
Diameter	51,118 km
	(30,775 miles)
Average distance from the sun	4,498 million km
	(2,795 million miles)
Rotation period	16.11 hours
Orbital period	164.9 years

Dwarf Planets

Dwarf planets are small, roundish objects in the Solar System. Like all the other objects in the Solar System, they also orbit the sun. Till date, **four dwarf planets** have been discovered. These are:

- Ceres
- Eris
- Pluto
- Makemake

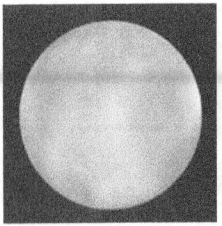 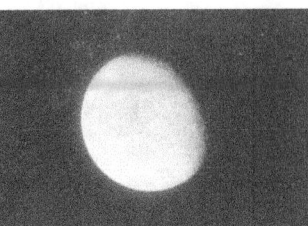 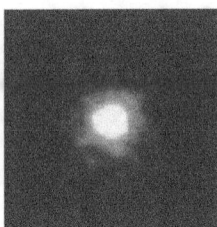 

While Ceres orbits between Jupiter and Mars, within the Main Belt of asteroids, Pluto and Eris orbit beyond Neptune as part of the Kuiper Belt. The Kuiper Belt is a belt made of ice and rocky objects.

Quick Facts

- The Sun contains about 99.86% of the mass in the Solar System. It is about 73% hydrogen, so most of the matter in the Solar System is hydrogen, with the remaining amount being mostly helium, oxygen and carbon. Everything else, like the metals and rocks is just a tiny fraction of a fraction of the mass in the Solar System.

- Since the Earth is constantly resurfacing itself, we can't find out how old it is, but there's another way to find out. Meteorites, which date back to the formation of the Solar System, have been raining down on Earth for millions of years. Scientists have sampled meteorites and learnt that they're all 4.6 billion years old. That means that everything in the Solar System formed are around the same time.

- Venus is the brightest planet in our sky and can sometimes be seen with the naked eye if you know where to look. It is the solar system's brightest planet -- yellow clouds of sulphuric acid reflect the sun's light brightly.

Chapter - 4

THE SUN

The Sun is in the *centre of our Solar System* and is one of the *biggest stars in our galaxy*. It is made up of *hot gases that glow*. These gases are kept together on the sun's surface with the help of gravity. A major portion of these gases, nearly three-quarters, is **hydrogen**. The rest is mostly **helium** along with very small quantities of nearly 90 other elements.

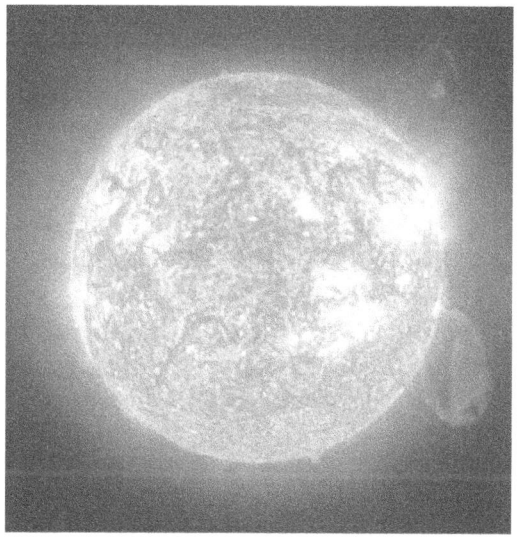

Size

The sun is about *1.4 million kilometres (8,70, 000 miles) in diameter*. It is the largest body in the Solar System. While 1.3 million earths can fit inside the sun, 109 earths could fit across its face. It is made up of about 3,30, 000 times more material than that of the earth.

Temperature

The sun is yellow in colour as its surface temperature is 5,500°C (9,900°F). While hotter stars are white in colour, the cooler ones are red. The core of the sun is 15 million°C (27 million°F). Here, 600 million tonnes of hydrogen is converted to helium every second with the help of nuclear reactions (the process of reacting various chemicals to produce nuclear energy).

Spicules

Spicules are short-lived jets of gas which look like *flames*. These leap to a height of *10,000 kilometres (6,200 miles)* from the surface of the sun.

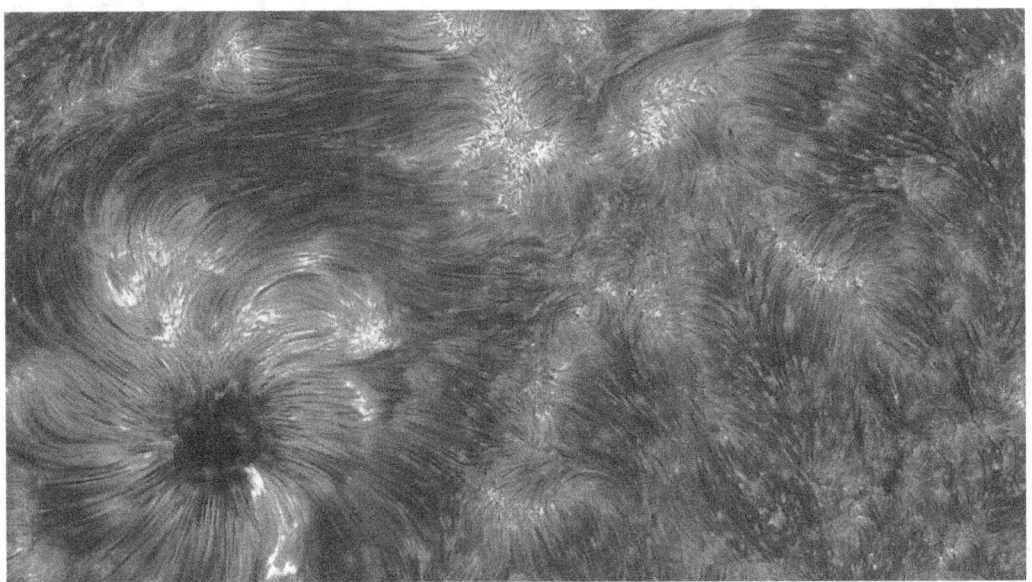

Atmosphere

The inner atmosphere of the sun, which lies directly above its surface, is known as the *chromosphere*. It extends to about *2,500 kilometres (1,550 miles)*. The chromosphere is followed by the *corona*. This extends to millions of kilometres into space.

Spin

As opposed to the spinning of the earth, different parts of the sun spin in different durations. While the regions near the poles take 30 days or more to complete one rotation, the equator completes it in 25 days.

Quick Facts

- If the sun is seen from Mercury, it appears 2.5 times bigger than what it looks from the earth.
- Jupiter takes almost 12 years to orbit the sun.
- The sun is at a distance of 149 million kilometres from the earth.
- The sun comprises about 25% helium and 75% hydrogen.
- The sun is responsible for the evaporation of about a trillion tons of water every day.
- A solar eclipse occurs when the moon is between the sun and the earth.
- The light from the sun reaches the earth in about eight minutes.
- The activity on the sun produces particles that are thrown out into space. This stream of particles, called the solar wind, consists primarily of protons and electrons and spreads throughout the solar system at about 450 km/sec. The solar wind has large effects on the tails of comets and the functioning of a spacecraft.
- Each second the sun loses 5 million tons of material and the sun's energy output is about 386 billion billion megawatts.

Chapter - 5

THE MOONS

All the planets in the Solar System, except Mercury and Venus, have their own satellites called the moons. There are more than 160 moons in the Solar System. All of these orbit around different planets.

The moons are of various sizes. Some are so huge that they are larger than Mercury, while some are only 2 kilometres (1.2 miles) across. Moons are generally made up of rock or rock and ice. Their surfaces have many impact craters (structures formed when a huge comet, asteroid or meteoroid crashes into a planet or a satellite). These were formed millions of years ago when the surface of the moons were hit by many asteroids (small solar bodies that orbit around the sun).

There are only nineteen moons in the Solar System that are more than 400 kilometres (250 miles) wide. While these moons are round in shape, smaller moons are irregular in shape.

The Moon

The earth's moon is the fifth largest of all the

moons in the Solar System. It is the earth's only natural satellite and is about a quarter the size of the earth. Its surface does not have water and is covered with *impact craters*.

IO

The most volcanic moon in the Solar System, *IO is very colourful*. Its surface is constantly renewed as molten rock erupts through its thin silicate-rock crust, and fast-moving columns of cold gas and frost grains shoot up from the surface cracks.

Europa

Europa is one of the four largest moons of Jupiter. The other three are *Io, Callisto* and *Ganymede*. Galileo Galilei was one of the first astronomers to see these four moons and so, together these four moons are called **Galileans**. Europa's surface has *brown grooves* that crisscross the blue-grey water ice.

Ganymede

Ganymede is the largest moon in the Solar System. It is one of Jupiter's moons and is about 5,262 kilometres (3,267 miles) in diameter. It is mainly made up of rock and ice, and has an *icy crust*. Till now, astronomers have found *63 moons around Jupiter*, but the number is increasing with astronomers finding more and more smaller moons.

Titan

Saturn has *60 moons* and *Titan is the largest of them all*. Its surface is made up of seas, methane lakes, dark plains and bright highlands. It is the only moon which has an atmosphere, which is rich in nitrogen gas.

Titania

Uranus has *27 moons* and *Titania is the largest of them all*. Titania, along with other large moons of Uranus, such as Miranda, Ariel, Umbriel and Oberon, have got their names from characters in English literature. Titania has a grey, icy surface, with a lot of impact craters and large cracks.

Triton

Out of Neptune's 13 moons, Triton is the largest. It is a ball made of rock and ice, with an icy surface. It is also called *cantaloupe* as its surface resembles a melon's skin.

Small Moons

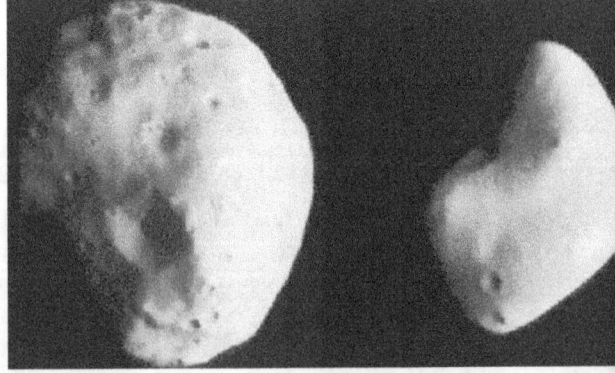

The Solar System has many small moons. Most of these are less than 400 kilometres (250 miles) across and irregular in shape. Quite a few of these have moons, such as the Mars has two moons, *Deimos* and *Phobos*, which started off as asteroids and later became moons.

Quick Facts

- It takes light about 1.5 seconds to reach the earth from the moon.
- The last man to land on the moon was Eugene Andrew Cernan in 1972.
- Neil Armstrong, the first person to walk on the moon, first put his left foot.
- A huge number of golf balls can be found on the moon as debris. Astronauts who have been to the moon and back used the balls for gravity experiments.
- The first person to walk on the moon was Neil Armstrong. The second was Edwin Aldrin.

Chapter - 6

THE METEORITES

Millions of tonnes of rocky matter enter the earth's atmosphere every year. Most of it originates from asteroids, but some comes from other comets, the Moon, and even the Mars. When these rocky materials come close to the earth, they are called **meteoroids**. Generally, this rocky matter burns up, but if it does survive and land, it is called a **meteorite**.

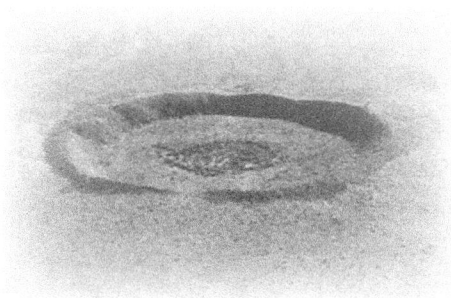

Meteorites are generally of the following three types:

- Stony meteorites
- Iron meteorites
- Stony-iron meteorites (extremely rare)

Meteor

Meteorites that burn in the atmosphere of the earth have *bright tails*. These short-lived streaks of light are termed as **meteors**, or **shooting stars**. About a million occur every day.

Esquel

Esquel is a rare stony-iron meteorite. It was found in 1951 in Esquel, Argentina. The iron-nickel metal of this meteorite has golden-coloured crystals of the olivine mineral embedded in it.

Thiel

Found in Antarctica, about 40 years ago, the Thiel Mountains have been formed by the stony-iron meteorites.

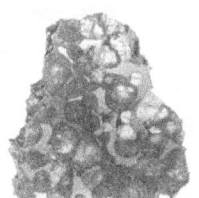

Murchison

Made up of water, minerals and various complex organic molecules, *Murchison is a stony meteorite*. It fell in *Australia in 1969* and has been thoroughly studied.

Barwell

In 1965, the *Barwell meteorite fell in England*. It was a part of a large shower of stones. When it entered the atmosphere of the earth, the friction caused the outer layer to heat up, and eventually, melt. After many years, it solidified and turned into a *black crust*.

Canyon Diablo

Canyon Diablo is an *iron meteorite*. It is a sliced and polished piece of the asteroid which was responsible for producing the *Barringer Crater*. Even though the pieces found are only a tiny portion of the asteroid, together they weigh about 30 tonnes.

Gibeon

After stony meteorites, iron meteorites are the second most commonly found. Gibeon is an *iron meteorite*. It is mainly made up of iron, but also has a small amount of *nickel* in it. It is one of the many *meteorites found in Namibia* since the 1830s.

Calcalong Creek

Quite a few of the meteorites found on the earth were formed when asteroids hit the moon. The *Calcalong Creek meteorite* is basically a *lunar surface soil* (soil that is found on the Moon) meteorite. It fell on the earth and turned into a rock due to the impact. It is located in *Australia*.

Nakhla

Nakhla is a *stony meteorite*. It is one of the many meteorites found on the earth that originated on Mars. It landed in Egypt on 28 June 1911, before which it spent millions of years in space after being blasted off from Mars.

Tektites

When a huge meteorite hits the earth, small glassy bodies can be formed. These are known as tektites.
Due to the impact, the surrounding earth rock disintegrates and melts, and then is thrown upwards. When it cools down and becomes hard, it falls back on the earth as *glassy pieces*.

Impact Craters

Craters are formed when meteorites crash into the earth. These are ususally very large in size. Formed about *50,000 years ago,* the Barringer Crater in *Arizona Desert, USA*, measures 1.2 kilometres (0.75 miles) across.

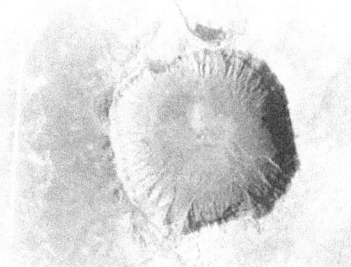

Quick Facts

- The asteroid belt is where the maximum meteorites come from.
- Meteorites fall under three major categories-Stone, iron and stone-iron.
- A meteorite is called a meteoroid before it enters the earth's atmosphere.
- The heaviest meteorite that fell on the earth weighed around 60 tonnes. It was called the Hoba West, and it fell in Africa.
- Meteor showers are periodic events. One can see thousands of meteors or shooting stars, as they are called, during such a shower. The most popular meteor showers are 'Perseids' (which peak around August 12) and 'Leonids' (which peak around November 17). During these showers, you can observe a shooting star at the rate of 1 meteor per minute on an average.
- Meteorites may look very much like earth rocks, or they may have a burnt appearance. They may be dense metallic chunks or more rocky. Some may have thumbprint-like depressions, roughened or smooth exteriors. They vary in size from micrometer size grains to large individual boulders.
- Some meteorites are sweet. They are made out of a substance similar to sugar.
- A falling meteor can travel at a speed of as much as 44 miles per second!
- Meteorites often contain minerals not found on the earth.

Chapter - 7

THE COMETS

The planetary region in the Solar System is surrounded by more than a *trillion comets*. Like planets, *comets also orbit the sun*. All the comets together form a vast sphere known as the **Oort Cloud**.

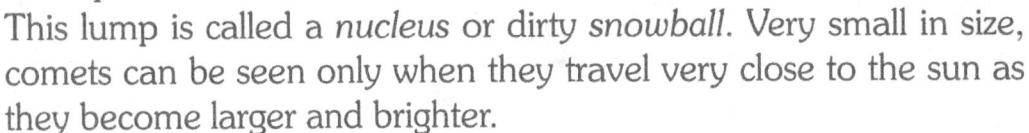

A comet is made up of a lump of *dirt and snow*. This lump is called a *nucleus* or dirty *snowball*. Very small in size, comets can be seen only when they travel very close to the sun as they become larger and brighter.

When a comet moves closer to the sun, it gets heated. All the snow in the comet starts turning into gas combined with the loose dust and begins to flow from the nucleus. When the comet passes closer to the sun than the orbit of Mars, this material forms a head (called a coma) and two tails, one of gas and one of dust.

Astronomers have identified more than **2,300 comets** that have passed through the sun's neighbourhood. While most of them just pass by, about 200 of these comets make return visits. Comets as magnificent as *Comet McNaught*, which was last seen in *January 2007*, can be seen only three to four times in a century.

Structure

The nucleus of a comet is made up of one-third rock dust and two-thirds snow.

Breaking up

The gravitational force of huge bodies, such as the Sun and Jupiter can pull a comet apart when it is passing them.

Quick Facts

- **Comets are in orbit around the sun as are our planets.**
- **Comets are remnants from the cold, outer regions of the Solar System, which have been formed about 4.5 billion years ago.**
- **Comet orbits are elliptical. It brings them close to the sun and takes them far away.**
- **Short period comets orbit the sun every 20 years or less. Long period comets orbit the sun every 200 years or longer. Those comets with orbits in between are called Halley-type comets.**

- Comets have three parts: the nucleus, the coma and the tails. The nucleus is the solid centre component made of ice, gas and rocky debris. The coma is the gas and dust atmosphere around the nucleus. The tails are formed when energy from the sun turns the coma so that it flows around the nucleus and forms a fanned out tail behind it extending millions of miles through space.
- We see a comet's coma and tail because sunlight reflects off the dust (in the coma and dust tail) and because the energy from the sun excites some molecules so that they glow and form a bluish tail called an ion tail and a yellow one made of neutral sodium atoms.

Chapter - 8

SPACE EXPLORATION

In the last five decades, humans have advanced technologically a great deal. They have been able to explore space with the help of spacecrafts. Within this short span of 50 years, more than 100 robotic crafts have been sent into space to explore the various components of the Solar System. These include the planets, stars, comets, asteroids, etc.

TIMELINE OF SPACE EXPLORATION

October 14, 1957

Russia launched the world's first artificial satellite, *Sputnik 1*, into the Earth's orbit.

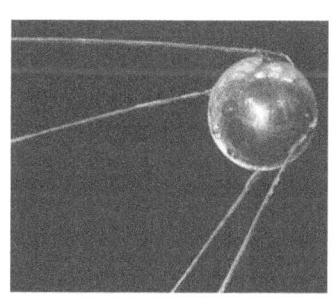

November 3, 1957

Sputnik 2 was launched into the Earth's orbit with a *Russian dog, Laika*, on board. This dog became the first creature to orbit the Earth.

January 2, 1959

Luna 1, a Russian spacecraft, became the first spacecraft to escape the Earth's gravity.

September 13, 1959

Russian spacecraft, Luna 2, was the first to land on the Moon. It crashed on its surface while landing.

April 12, 1961

Yuri Gagarin, a Russian astronaut, *became the first person to travel in space*. His flight lasted for about 108 minutes.

June 16, 1963

Valentina Tereshkova, a Russian astronaut, *became the first woman to go into the space.*

March 18, 1965

Another Russian astronaut, *Alexei Leonov*, became the first person to spacewalk (an astronaut's movement in the space outside the aircraft). Spacewalk is also known as Extra Vehicular Activity (EVA).

February 3, 1966

Luna 9, the space shuttle that successfully landed on the Moon.

December 24, 1968

US spacecraft *Apollo 8* became the first manned mission that left the Earth's gravity and orbited the Moon.

July 20, 1969

Neil Armstrong and Buzz Aldrin of Apollo 11 became the first human beings to walk on the Moon.

April 19, 1971

Russia launched the first space station – *Salyut 1*.

December 3, 1973

Pioneer 10, a US spacecraft, became the first craft to fly by Jupiter.

March 29, 1974

Mariner 10, another US spacecraft, became the first craft to fly by Mercury.

July 17, 1975

US craft *Apollo 18* and Russian *Soyuz 19* made the first international space rendezvous.

October 22, 1975

The first images from the surface of Venus were transmitted by the Russian spacecraft, *Venera 9*.

July 20, 1976

Viking 1, a US spacecraft, successfully landed on Mars.

September 1, 1979

US spacecraft *Pioneer 11* became the first to fly by Saturn.

April 12, 1981

Columbia, the first US space shuttle, was launched.

Launching of the first US space shuttle, Columbia

January 24, 1986

Voyager 2, a US craft, became the first to fly by Uranus.

February 20, 1986

The first module of Russian space station Mir was launched into orbit.

March 13, 1986

Giotto, a European spacecraft, became the first to take a close-up look at a comet.

August 24, 1989

The Hubble Space Telescope was launched.

September 15, 1990

Magellan, a US spacecraft, began a three-year mapping programme of planet Venus.

October 29, 1991

Galileo, a US spacecraft, made the first flyby of an asteroid as it passed Gaspra.

July 13, 1995

US spacecraft *Galileo* arrived at Jupiter. It then released a probe to enter Jupiter's atmosphere.

July 4, 1997

Mars Pathfinder, a US spacecraft, and its Sojourner rover landed on Mars.

November 20, 1998

The first module of the International Space Station (ISS), *Zarya*, was launched.

February 12, 2001

The Near Earth Asteroid Rendezvous (NEAR) Spacecraft landed on asteroid, *Eros*.

August 25, 2003

Spitzer, an infrared space telescope, was launched into the Earth's orbit.

December 25, 2003

Mars Express, Europe's first interplanetary craft, became the first to orbit Mars.

January 4, 2004

Mars Exploration Rover Spirit landed on Mars. It was followed by its twin, Opportunity.

March 2, 2004

Rosetta, a European spacecraft, began its journey to Comet Churyumov-Gerasimenko. This journey would last for 10 years and carried lander Philae.

June 30, 2004

Cassini, a US craft, arrived at Saturn. The main aim of this journey was not only to study the planet, but also its moons. It released Huygens to land on the moon Titan.

November 20, 2005

Hayabusa, a Japanese spacecraft, landed on asteroid Itokawa.

January 19, 2006

New Horizons, a US craft, was launched on a journey to Pluto, which would last for eight years.

August 4, 2007

Phoenix, a US spacecraft, began its journey for Mars. It arrived there in 2008.

January 14, 2008

Messenger, a US spacecraft, made its *first flyby of Mercury*. This was a preparation before sending a craft to orbit the planet in 2011.

Quick Facts

- There is no set number of people in an astronaut candidate class. The NASA selects its candidates on an as-needed basis. To even apply to be an astronaut, candidates must have completed 1,000 hours of flying time in a jet aircraft.
- A spacesuit weighs approximately 280 pounds—without the astronaut—and it takes about 45 minutes to put it on.
- Snoopy, from the Peanuts Comics, is the astronauts' personal safety mascot.
- Explorer 1, launched on January 31, 1958, was the first artificial satellite sent into space by the United States. It orbited the Earth every 115 minutes, and its cargo included a cosmic ray detector designed to measure the radiation environment in the Earth's orbit.

RAPIDEX ENGLISH SPEAKING COURSE/EXCEL ENGLISH SPEAKING COURSE

ISBN : 9789381448908
(Telugu)

ISBN : 9789381448915
(Bangla)

ISBN : 9789381448922
(Oriya)

ISBN : 9789381448939
(Assamese)

ISBN : 9789381448946
(Nepalese)

Published in sixteen languages
Hindi, Malayalam, Tamil, Telugu, Kannada, Marathi, Gujarati, Bangla, Oriya, Urdu, Assamese, Punjabi, Nepalese, Persian, Arabic and Sinhalese

REGIONAL LANGUAGE/SPOKEN ENGLISH/LEARNING COURSES

ISBN : 9789357940054
(Bangla)

ISBN : 9789357940016
(Bangla)

ISBN :9789357940023
(Bangla)

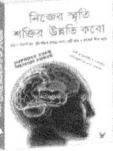
ISBN : 9789357940085
(Bangla)

ISBN : 9789357940825
(Bangla)

ISBN : 9789357940092
(Bangla)

ISBN : 9789357940009
(Bangla)

ISBN : 9789357940030
(Bangla)

ISBN : 9789357941303
(2 Colour Book)

ISBN : 9789357940061
(Bangla)

ISBN : 9789357940047
(Bangla)

ISBN : 9788122310924
(Bangla)

ISBN : 9789357940078
(Bangla)

ISBN 9789350570357
(Kannada)

ISBN : 9789350571200
(Kannada)

ISBN : 9789350570340
(Kannada)

ISBN : 9789350570944
(Kannada)

(Coming Soon)
Marathi

ISBN : 9789350570951
(Kannada)

ISBN : 9789350571309
(Kannada)

ISBN : 9789350571828
(Gujarati)

ISBN : 9789350571781
(Gujarati)

ISBN : 9789350571811
(Marathi)

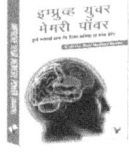
ISBN : 9789350571804
(Marathi)

ISBN : 9789381384138
(Tamil)

ISBN : 9789381384121
(Tamil)

(Coming Soon)
Punjabi

ISBN : 9789357940153
(Eng.-Bangla)

ISBN : 9789357940399
(Eng.-Kannada)

ISBN : 9789357940375
(Eng.-Odia)

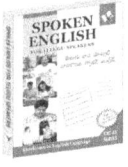
ISBN : 9789357940382
(Eng.-Telugu)

ISBN : 9789357941358
(Eng.-Malayalam)

ISBN : 9789357941327
(Eng.-Tamil)

ISBN : 9789357940856
(Eng.-Marathi)

ISBN : 9789357940849
(Eng.-Gujarati)

(Coming Soon)
Kannada

ISBN : 9789357941334
(Eng.-Assamese)

ISBN : 9789357941341
(Eng.-Urdu)

ISBN : 9789350570760
(Telugu)

ISBN : 9789350570098
(Telugu)

ISBN : 9789350571699
(Bangla)

ISBN : 9789350571125
(Bangla)

ISBN : 9789357940146
(Kannada)

ISBN : 9789357940139
(Kannada)

(Coming Soon)
Gujarati

ISBN : 9789350571620
(Odia)

ISBN : 9789350571118
(Odia)

ISBN : 9789350570982
(Marathi)

ISBN : 9789350571835
(Marathi)

ISBN : 9789357940795
Bangla

ISBN : 9789357940801
Odia

ISBN : 9789357940818
Telugu

All Books Available on Flipkart, Amazon, Infibeam, Snapdeal, Shopcluse • marketing@vspublishers.com

V&S OLYMPIAD SERIES FOR CLASSES 1-10

MATHS OLYMPIAD (CLASS 1-10)

ISBN : 9789357940504   ISBN : 9789357940511   ISBN : 9789357940528   ISBN : 9789357940535   ISBN : 9789357940542

ISBN : 9789357940559   ISBN : 9789357940566   ISBN : 9789357940573   ISBN : 9789357940580   ISBN : 9789357940597

SCIENCE OLYMPIAD (CLASS 1-10)

ISBN : 9789357940405   ISBN : 9789357940412   ISBN : 9789357940429   ISBN : 9789357940436   ISBN : 9789357940443

ISBN : 9789357940450   ISBN : 9789357940467   ISBN : 9789357940474   ISBN : 9789357940481   ISBN : 9789357940498

CYBER OLYMPIAD (CLASS 1-10)

ISBN : 9789357942102   ISBN : 9789357940603   ISBN : 9789357940610   ISBN : 9789357940627   ISBN : 9789357940634

ISBN : 9789357940641   ISBN : 9789357940658   ISBN : 9789357940665   ISBN : 9789357940672   ISBN : 9789357940689

ENGLISH OLYMPIAD (CLASS 1-10)

ISBN : 9789357940696   ISBN : 9789357940702   ISBN : 9789357940719   ISBN : 9789357940726   ISBN : 9789357940733

ISBN : 9789357940740   ISBN : 9789357940757   ISBN : 9789357940764   ISBN : 9789357940771   ISBN : 9789357940788

OLYMPIAD ONLINE TEST PACKAGE (CLASS 1-10)

ISBN : 9789357941754   ISBN : 9789357941761   ISBN : 9789357941778   ISBN : 9789357941785

ISBN : 9789357941792   ISBN : 9789357941808   ISBN : 9789357941815   ISBN : 9789357941822

ISBN : 9789357941839   ISBN : 9789357941846

OLYMPIAD ONLINE TEST PACKAGE CLASS 1-10
with CD with Activation Voucher
web Portal: www.vsexamprep.com

OLYMPIAD COMBO PACK (4 BOOK SET)

ISBN : 9789357942003   ISBN : 9789357942010   ISBN : 9789357942027

ISBN : 9789357942034   ISBN : 9789357942041   ISBN : 9789357942058

ISBN : 9789357942065   ISBN : 9789357942072   ISBN : 9789357942089

 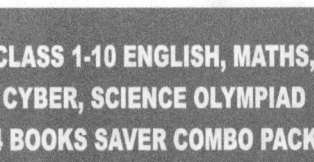

ISBN : 9789357942096

CLASS 1-10 ENGLISH, MATHS, CYBER, SCIENCE OLYMPIAD 4 BOOKS SAVER COMBO PACK

All Books Available on Flipkart, Amazon, Infibeam, Snapdeal, Shopcluse • marketing@vspublishers.com

www.ingramcontent.com/pod-product-compliance
Lightning Source LLC
LaVergne TN
LVHW081355060426
835510LV00013B/1842